WHIT'S END

MEALTIME
DEVOTIONS

HOME SWEET HOME

FOCUS ON THE FAMILY PRESENTS

Adventures in ODYSSEY®

WHIT'S END
MEALTIME DEVOTIONS

HOME SWEET HOME

Tyndale House Publishers, Inc.
Carol Stream, Illinois

90 FAITH-BUILDING IDEAS YOUR KIDS WILL EAT UP!

JOHN AVERY WHITTAKER
WITH HELP FROM CRYSTAL BOWMAN AND TRICIA GOYER

Whit's End Mealtime Devotions
Copyright © 2013 Focus on the Family

A Focus on the Family book published by Tyndale House Publishers, Inc., Carol Stream, Illinois 60188

Focus on the Family and Adventures in Odyssey, and the accompanying logos and designs, are federally registered trademarks of Focus on the Family, Colorado Springs, CO 80995.

This book was previously published by Focus on the Family as *Mealtime Moments*, © 2000.

TYNDALE and Tyndale's quill logo are registered trademarks of Tyndale House Publishers, Inc.

Editor: Marianne Hering
Cover design by Jacqueline L. Nuñez
Cover illustration and interior illustrations of characters by Gary Locke
Interior design by Lexie Rhodes

ISBN: 978-1-58997-676-4

Printed in the United States of America
1 2 3 4 5 6 7 8 9 /18 17 16 15 14 13

For manufacturing information regarding this product, please call 1-800-323-9400.

Contents

Holiday Devotions

Theme Devotions

How to Use This Book

by John Avery Whittaker

There are a lot of surveys by reputable organizations demonstrating the importance of consistent mealtimes for families. But those of us who grew up with consistent mealtimes at home don't need surveys to tell us how important those times were. To sit down together, to share food, to talk about how our days went, to explore our joys and pains as a family, were invaluable not only to our health and wellbeing, but also to our relationships as a family. I can easily understand why the Bible talks about mealtimes as often as it does. And God used mealtimes to teach His people—from Moses teaching his people about the Passover to Jesus teaching His disciples at the Last Supper.

In both the Passover and the Last Supper, we can see how conversation, and even the food itself, was used to grab everyone's attention and give the items around the table a deeper eternal meaning. Though those original occasions were somber, they have also become sources of joy and fun for everyone involved.

That's the point of this book: to turn mealtimes into lively times for talk and teaching about the Christian life. It's laid out to make family conversation as easy as pie for you to do. Here's the recipe for meaningful mealtimes (and, yes, the puns are intentional):

After announcing the title, read the Mealtime Prayer suggestion and then ask your children to pray it together.

Then read the Appetizer. The Appetizer is just that—something to whet your appetite for more.

Follow it with the Main Course. This contains the "meat" of the section.

Once you've given your family something to chew on, it's time for Table Talk. These challenging questions will help your kids think about what they've just learned and explain how to digest it for their daily lives.

Finally, end with Vitamins and Minerals—a Bible verse that relates to the day's reading and discussion.

To get the most out of this book, allow yourself to be *flexible*. You don't have to go through it from cover to cover. You might want to use the table of contents to find a topic that relates to what's happening in your family on that day.

Besides these regular readings—some of which are anything but ordinary—we've included extra sections: Holidays and Special Occasions and Theme Meals. Kids will especially enjoy these. Be sure to leaf through those sections in advance so you know what's coming up. Plus, a few of them require a minimal amount of preparation, just to add to the fun.

The point is to turn mealtimes into a fun and enjoyable time of learning about each other and about bringing God into every part of our lives. Be sensitive to how your children respond. Allow enough time for them to answer the questions, but don't force conversation if they don't seem interested. That usually isn't a problem with kids, I've found. These readings have been time-tested around a few tables and should stir up animated conversations about the things that really matter.

Have fun!

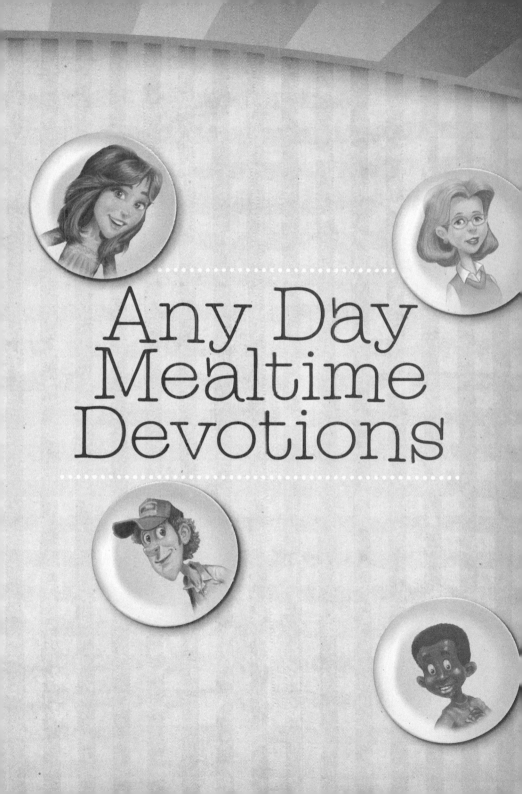

Any Day
Mealtime
Devotions

Bull's-Eye

Mealtime Prayer:
Thank God that He is always with us and that we never have to be afraid.

Appetizer:
The giant Goliath was over nine feet tall. How many people from your family would have to stand on each other's shoulders to be as tall as Goliath?

Goliath's armor weighed about 125 pounds. How many kids in your family could Goliath have picked up to equal that weight?

Main Course:
Imagine facing a giant in battle. What weapons would you want to help you? David, a young shepherd boy, was brave enough to fight a giant. Read the exciting story of David and Goliath in 1 Samuel 17:17–51.

Table Talk:
- What did David take to help him fight Goliath?
- Where did David get his courage?
- What would you have done if you were David?
- What kinds of giants do you face in your everyday life?
- What can you do when you're afraid?

Vitamins and Minerals:
[Moses said,] "Be strong and courageous. Do not be afraid or terrified because of [your enemies], for the LORD your God goes with you; he will never leave you nor forsake you" (Deuteronomy 31:6).

Water, Water Everywhere

Mealtime Prayer:

After the leader prays each phrase, everyone says, *"We thank You, dear Lord."*

> *Leader: "For food to eat and water to drink,*
> *For healthy bodies and minds that think,*
> *For all that we have and all we enjoy,*
> *For every girl and every boy."*

Appetizer:

Try to come up with 10 uses for water. Go!

Main Course:

Eat as much of your dinner as you can without taking a drink. How long could you last?

Why do we need to drink? What makes us thirsty? When do you most appreciate an ice-cold glass of water?

Table Talk:

- Jesus is called the *Living Water*. How is He like water? Why do we need Him?
- Where can we find *living water*? How can we drink *living water*?
- Why does the satisfaction of *living water* last forever?

Vitamins and Minerals:

[Jesus said,] "Whoever drinks the water I give him will never thirst. Indeed, the water I give him will become in him a spring of water welling up to eternal life" (John 4:14).

Time-Out

Mealtime Prayer:

Thank God for times to rest and worship. Thank Him for your church, the minister, and the leaders of your church.

Appetizer:

What would happen if people worked every day and never took a day off? Why do we need a day of rest?

Main Course:

What different types of churches have you been to? What is your favorite place of worship? Why do we need to take time to worship God?

Table Talk:

- In the Ten Commandments, God tells us to remember the Sabbath day to keep it holy. What does that mean? (Read Exodus 20:8–11.)
- What did God do on the seventh day after He created the world? If God doesn't get tired, why did He take a day off?
- Think of 10 good reasons to go to church.

Vitamins and Minerals:

Let [God's people] exalt him in the assembly of the people and praise him in the council of the elders (Psalm 107:32).

You've Got Mail!

Mealtime Prayer:
Name some missionaries you know. Ask God to bless and protect them, as well as other missionaries throughout the world.

Appetizer:
Have you ever read a letter from a missionary? When was the last time you wrote a letter on paper or in electronic form? When was the last time you received one?

If someone collected your letters and put them in a book, what kind of book would it be: mystery, adventure, drama, comedy?

Main Course:
What is the most famous collection of letters ever written? (Hint: They're in the Bible.) The apostle Paul became a missionary, traveling to many places, from Rome to Syria, to tell people about Jesus. He didn't stay in one place very long, so he wrote 13 letters (now in the New Testament) to keep in touch with the new Christians. Why do you think he wanted to keep in touch with them?

Table Talk:
- Would anyone besides the friend you've written to be interested in your letters?
- How are Paul's letters different from yours?
- Paul's letters are messages from God to you. How should you treat them?

Vitamins and Minerals:
I thank my God every time I remember you (Philippians 1:3).

Plain Ol' Vanilla

Mealtime Prayer:
Let each person offer his or her own kind of prayer—short or long, silent or aloud. Have the last person thank God for your different tastes in prayer—and food!

Appetizer:
Which ice-cream flavor is the top seller: Strawberry, Cookies 'N' Cream, Chocolate, or Vanilla? (Answer: Vanilla)[1] What's your favorite flavor?

Main Course:
Why isn't there just one flavor of ice cream? If you were ice cream, which flavor would you want to be: Mysterious Mocha, Cheery Cherry, Quiet Kiwi, Grumpy Grape, or Outrageous Orange? Why?

Why didn't God make just one kind of person? Every one of us has different "tastes." Your flavor is what makes you *you*.

Each of us has a different way of praying and worshipping God, too. Some like to sing praises. Some are champs at quoting Bible verses. Others would rather sit quietly and think about God's goodness. All of these are part of your flavor.

Table Talk:
Take a vote on the following questions:
- Would you rather sing a praise song with motions or without? Why?
- Would you rather pray standing up, sitting, kneeling, or bowing with your face to the floor? Why?
- Now that you've voted, should you all have to sing and pray in the ways that got the most votes? Why or why not?

Vitamins and Minerals:
There are different kinds of service, but the same Lord (1 Corinthians 12:5).

---

1 "Ice Cream Sales and Trends," International Dairy Foods Association, 2012, http://www.idfa.org/news--views/media-kits/ice-cream/ice-cream-sales-and-trends/.

Soul Food

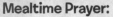

Mealtime Prayer:
(Tune: "Amazing Grace")

> "*Amazing grace, how great Thou art, You meet my every need.*
> *You quench my thirst, You guard my home, my soul and body feed.*"

Appetizer:
Did you know it can take as long as 24 hours for a meal to get through your digestive system?[1] That's because your small intestines are four or five times taller than you are![2] Look around and find something that tall. Would it fit inside you?

Main Course:
How is the phrase "you are what you eat" true? What happens to your body when you eat nutritious food?

Besides food, what other things do you feed on throughout the day (television, music, friends, etc.)? Which of these please God? Do these things strengthen you or weaken you? How?

One good thing you can feed on is the Bible. God's Word can be thought of as food for your soul. Why does absorbing God's truths into your life give you strength?

Table Talk:
- Name five things you can "absorb" from the Bible. How do they become a part of you?
- What sort of music feeds the soul?
- What sort of music, movies, or games hurt your soul? Why?

Vitamins and Minerals:
You are strong, and the word of God lives in you (1 John 2:14).

---

1. Dr. Michael F. Picco, "Digestion: How Long Does It Take?" Mayo Clinic, 2010 http://www.mayoclinic.com/health/digestive-system/an00896.
2. "Picture of the Intestines," WebMD, http://www.webmd.com/digestive-disorders/picture-of-the-intestines.

King-Sized Oven

Mealtime Prayer:
Thank God for the many ways He takes care of us. Ask Him to give you the courage to obey Him.

Appetizer:
You've probably said, "I'd give anything for a soda!" or "I'd die for an ice-cream cone." What would you be willing to die for? Chocolate mousse? To score a winning goal? Your beliefs?

Main Course:
Three young men were willing to die just to stand up for their God. Or were they? Read the thrilling story of three brave men from Daniel 3:1–6, 12–13, 16–18, 21, 26–28.

Table Talk:
- What was the most exciting part of the story?
- What were they willing to die for?
- Do you think the three men knew they would not burn up? Why or why not?
- What should you do when someone wants you to disobey God?

Vitamins and Minerals:
[Peter and John said,] "For we cannot help speaking about what we have see and heard" (Acts 4:18–20).

Attitude of Gratitude

Mealtime Prayer:
What are some things that your family members have done for each other today? Thank God for your family and the ways you can help one another.

Appetizer:
How do you feel when you do something nice for someone else, and he or she doesn't thank you for what you've done? Have you ever forgotten to thank someone for doing something nice for you?

Main Course:
The Bible tells us that one day Jesus healed 10 men who were sick with a disease called leprosy (Luke 17:12–19). Only one of the men took time to thank Jesus for healing him. How do you think Jesus felt about this? Why do you think the other nine men didn't thank Jesus?

Why is it important to say thank you to our friends and family for things they do for us? Why is it important to thank God for what He does?

Table Talk:
- What things do you take for granted but should be thankful for?
- How does it help your relationships when you remember to show gratitude?
- Write a thank-you note to someone, and give it to him or her tomorrow.

Vitamins and Minerals:
Give thanks to the LORD, call on his name; make known among the nations what he has done (Psalm 105:1).

Sweet as Honey

Mealtime Prayer:

"Dear Lord Jesus, may the things I say come out as words that please You and express care for others."

Appetizer:

Have each person taste a drop or two of honey. How does it taste? When someone calls you "Honey," does it mean that

    a. you are thick and syrupy?

    b. you were made by bees?

    c. you are sweet and pleasant?

    d. you belong on a biscuit?

Main Course:

There is a saying that goes "Sticks and stones may break my bones, but words will never hurt me." Is it true? Why or why not?

How can words hurt us? How can our words hurt others?

The Bible says that pleasant words are sweet as honey and healing to the bones. How can words be sweet? How can they be healing?

Table Talk:

- Why does God want you to use sweet words?
- What should you do if your words have hurt someone?
- Say something kind to someone at your table.
- What kind words can you say to someone tomorrow? (Be sure to do it.)

Vitamins and Minerals:

Pleasant words are a honeycomb, sweet to the soul and healing to the bones (Proverbs 16:24).

True or False?

Mealtime Prayer:
Thank God for the Bible and the messages He gives us in His Word.

Appetizer:
Each person should think of a message, true or false, that he or she wants to give. It could be "Mom is beautiful," "Lions eat flowers," or anything. Everyone then shares his or her message. The rest of you decide whether the message is true or false.

Main Course:
How did you decide which messages were true or false? When someone tells us something, how can we know whether he or she is telling us the truth?

The Bible includes many messages. Prophets wrote some messages about things that were going to take place in the future. How did the prophets know what to write? How can we know whether they were true?

For example, the prophet Isaiah predicted that the Messiah would be born. Was this true? (See Isaiah 9:6.) Why or why not? How do we know that everything in the Bible is true?

Table Talk:
- What is your favorite message in the Bible?
- What message in the Bible has not yet come true?

Vitamins and Minerals:
The prophet who prophesies peace will be recognized as one truly sent by the LORD only if his prediction comes true (Jeremiah 28:9).

Kids Rule!

Mealtime Prayer:
Pray for the leaders of our country; pray that they would be good examples and do right in the sight of God.

Appetizer:
Who is probably the youngest teacher whom you know? Do you know any young pastors? Who was the youngest man to become president of the United States? (Answer: Theodore Roosevelt at age 42)[1] If you became president, what changes would you make? Why?

Main Course:
Choose a child to be the leader for five minutes. He or she will tell the others what to eat and when to eat. (You may want to let children take turns.)

How does being the leader feel? How does it feel when you are not the leader? Which would you rather be? Why?

A boy named Josiah became the king and leader of Judah when he was only eight years old. The Bible tells us that Josiah did right in the sight of the Lord (2 Kings 22:2). What do you think that means?

Table Talk:
- How can you be a good leader at home? With your friends?
- How could you help the country serve God? (Hint: See the Vitamins and Minerals.)

Vitamins and Minerals:
The Lord appeared to [Solomon] at night and said: ". . . If my people, who are called by my name, will humble themselves and pray and seek my face and turn from their wicked ways, then will I hear from heaven and will forgive their sin and will heal their land" (2 Chronicles 7:12, 14).

---

1   John Roach, "Who Knew? US Presidential Trivia," National Geographic News, 2004, http://news.nationalgeographic.com/news/2004/08/0823_040823_presidentialtrivia.html.

Dirty Dishes

Mealtime Prayer:
Choose someone to read the following prayer:
> *"Thank You, Father, for the food You give us every day.*
> *Thank You for forgiving us and washing our sins away. Amen."*

Appetizer:
Count how many dishes are on your table, including the utensils. How clean are they?

Main Course:
After you finish your meal, describe what the dishes and utensils look like. Can you tell what you had to eat by what's sticking to the plate? Which food made the most mess? By looking at the empty glasses, can you tell what you had to drink? Why do you wash the dishes, glasses, and utensils before using them again?

Table Talk:
- How does your life become dirty and messy like the dinner dishes?
- Could someone tell where you've been or what you've done by looking at your life or listening to you?
- If you're a "dirty dish," how can you get clean?
- How can you stay clean?

Vitamins and Minerals:
Create in me a pure heart, O God, and renew a steadfast spirit within me (Psalm 51:10).

Lost and Found

Mealtime Prayer:
Tell God how thankful you are that He takes care of you as a shepherd cares for and watches over his sheep.

Appetizer:
Sheep are curious but dumb animals. Did you know that sheep are often unable to find their way home even if the sheepfold is within sight? Knowing this, the shepherd never takes his eyes off his wandering sheep. Read Psalm 32:8.

Main Course:
Set the table with one less plate than needed. Hide the plate, and then ask your family to look for it. Celebrate when you find it.

Read the story in Luke 15:4–7. Jesus told about finding something that was lost. What does *repent* mean? Why should we celebrate when a person repents?

Table Talk:
- Why does God look for lost people?
- Why was the plate important? Why was the sheep important? Why is each person important?
- Why do you think Jesus used stories to tell us about His kingdom? How do these stories help us understand?

Vitamins and Minerals:
We had to celebrate and be glad, because this brother of yours was dead and is alive again; he was lost and is found (Luke 15:32).

Company's Coming!

Mealtime Prayer:

"Lord Jesus, be our holy guest,
Our morning joy, our evening rest,
And with our daily bread impart
Your love and peace to every heart. Amen."[1]

Appetizer:

Did you know that in the White House, the State Dining Room can seat 140 people? Theodore Roosevelt decorated that room with hunting trophies and hung a moose head over the fireplace![2] If your parents let you, how would you decorate your dining room?

Main Course:

What would you do if the president of the United States were coming to your house for dinner? What would you fix?

We have someone even more important than the president "visiting" us every day. Who? If you have an extra chair, set a place for the King of Kings.

Table Talk:

- How can you daily prepare your heart for God's presence?
- How can you make God a special part your daily life, including mealtimes?
- If Jesus were at your table, what would you serve for dessert?

Vitamins and Minerals:

[Jesus said,] "Here I am! I stand at the door and knock. If anyone hears my voice and opens the door, I will come in and eat with him, and he with me" (Revelation 3:20).

---

1. Christopher Health: sparky@camtech.net.au.
2. "Inside the White House: Décor and Art," Whitehouse.gov, http://www.whitehouse.gov/about/inside-white-house/rooms; "Historic Photographs," The White House Historical Association, Photograph 6, http://www.whitehousehistory.org/whha_photographs/whitehouse_national-photo.html.

The Greatest Commandment

Mealtime Prayer:

> *"I'll try my best to live this day,*
> *By the Golden Rule in every way!*
> *Amen."*

Appetizer:

Did you know that "Love your neighbor as yourself" is sometimes called the Golden Rule? Why is it "golden"? Bible authors showed love by listening to God and sharing His Word.

Main Course:

What would happen if you bought a new kitchen appliance and no directions were included? Would you be able to use it safely? Why are directions important? How did God give us His directions? What are His instructions for?

For any kitchen appliance, the two most important directions may be (1) remember to plug it in, and (2) do not stick your fingers in any moving parts—ouch! What are the two most important directions of the Bible? Read Matthew 22:37–39.

Table Talk:

- What one word will help you remember the two most important directions?
- What does loving God this way look like?
- How can you love your family right now?

Vitamins and Minerals:

Jesus replied: " 'Love the Lord your God with all your heart and with all your soul and with all your mind.' This is the first and greatest commandment. And the second is like it: 'Love your neighbor as yourself' " (Matthew 22:37–39).

Need an Eraser?

Mealtime Prayer:
Thank God for your meal and praise God that He is perfect and never makes mistakes.

Appetizer:
Have someone get a pencil for everyone to look at. Which end of the pencil is used for writing? What is the other end used for? Why do we need both ends of the pencil?

Main Course:
What things besides pencil writing do you wish you could erase? Why? Does God ever need an "eraser"? What are some perfect things that God has done?

Table Talk:
- How does knowing that God is perfect help you?
- If God is perfect, why isn't the world?
- If God knows you are not perfect, what do you think He expects from you?
- What did Jesus, God's Son, do that is similar to an eraser?

Vitamins and Minerals:
I will proclaim the name of the LORD. Oh, praise the greatness of our God! He is the Rock, his works are perfect, and all his ways are just (Deuteronomy 32:3–4).

Be a Bookworm

Mealtime Prayer:
Have someone read the following prayer:
> *"Your Word, O Lord, teaches me truth.*
> *Your Word shows me the way.*
> *Help me to learn; help me to listen.*
> *Help me, O Lord, to obey. Amen."*

Appetizer:
Name the books each of you has read in the past week or month. What kind of books do you enjoy reading the most? Why? If someone said he would put you in prison for reading a certain book, what would you do?

Main Course:
The Bible is an all-time best seller! Why do you think so many people read it? What are some things we can learn from reading the Bible? How is the Bible different from other books?

Table Talk:
- How important is the Bible to you? Why? Would you read it even if you'd go to prison? (This is a real possibility in some countries.)
- How can reading the Bible help you make decisions every day?
- If you believe what the Bible says, how should that affect how you treat others?
- Why is it important to memorize Bible verses?

Vitamins and Minerals:
I have hidden your word in my heart that I might not sin against you (Psalm 119:11).

Caterpillar or Butterfly?

Mealtime Prayer:
Thank God for His salvation and that He changes lives.

Appetizer:
The caterpillar spins its cocoon with silk. What other creature spins with silk?
(Answer: The spider spins its web with silk.)

Main Course:
A caterpillar is not always a caterpillar. It eats and eats until it is full. Then it spins a silky cocoon around itself and goes to sleep. When it wakes up and comes out of its cocoon, it is a new creature—a butterfly.

If you could go to sleep and wake up different, what would you be? Why?

How was Saul in the New Testament like a caterpillar? Read Acts 9:1–22 to find out.

Table Talk:
- Are you a caterpillar or a butterfly? Why?
- How do people change when they become Christians?
- When you meet someone, how can you tell if he or she is a Christian?
- How can people tell that you are a Christian?

Vitamins and Minerals:
If anyone is in Christ, he is a new creation; the old has gone, the new has come! (2 Corinthians 5:17).

Nicknames

Mealtime Prayer:

Have someone read the following prayer:

"Dear Father, You are Lord and King, almighty Creator of everything. Messiah, Counselor, Prince of Peace, may Your blessings never cease. Amen."

Appetizer:

Reverse the first and last letters of your name. What do you get? (Examples: Mark = Karm, Chris = Shric.)

Main Course:

Do you have a nickname? If so, what is it? Do your parents ever call you "honey," "buddy," or "sweetie pie"? What other names do they call you? Why do we have nicknames?

Some people have titles that refer to their jobs, such as doctor or officer. Think of other names or titles that describe what people do.

God has many different names too. Some of God's names describe His character or what He's like, such as holy and almighty. What are some other names that describe God?

Some of God's names describe what He does, such as Creator or Savior. What are some other names that describe what God does?

Table Talk:

- Why do you think God has so many names?
- Using the letters of the alphabet, think of more names for God (for example, A = Almighty).
- If you had to choose a nickname to describe yourself, what would it be? Why?

Vitamins and Minerals:

And he will be called Wonderful Counselor, Mighty God, Everlasting Father, Prince of Peace (Isaiah 9:6).

Bread of Life

Mealtime Prayer:
Thank God for the many ways He provides for you. Thank Him for being the Bread of Life.

Appetizer:
Name all the different kinds of bread that you can think of. What is your favorite?

Main Course:
Have everyone at the table eat a piece of bread. How does it taste? What do you like with it (butter, cheese, liver, ketchup, etc.)?

Breads in various forms are eaten all over the world by almost everyone. Why do so many people eat bread? What are some of the different ways people use bread? (For example, in Ethiopia they use it as a utensil!) How is it good for us?

The Bible says that Jesus is the Bread of Life. What do you think that means? How is the "Bread of Life" different from regular bread?

Table Talk:
- Where can you find the bread that Jesus has to offer?
- How do you fill yourself with the Bread of Life? How is this bread good for you?
- How can you offer the Bread of Life to others?

Vitamins and Minerals:
[Jesus said,] "I tell you the truth, he who believes has everlasting life. I am the bread of life" (John 6:47–48).

Not by Bread Alone

Mealtime Prayer:
Thank God for at least three ways He provides for you besides food.

Appetizer:
If you had the power to do so, what food would you make appear before you right now?

Main Course:
Have you ever been really, really hungry? When? What was it like? Once, Jesus went 40 days and 40 nights without food! Imagine how hungry He must have been. How would you handle that kind of hunger?

The Devil thought that would be the perfect time to trick Jesus. Read Matthew 4:1–4. How did Jesus answer Satan? Why do you think it worked? How do you think Satan feels about the Bible? Why?

Table Talk:

- Think of a time you were tempted. How did you handle it? How well did it work?
- How could you handle temptation like Jesus did?
- How can knowing the Bible help you?

Vitamins and Minerals:
For everything that was written in the past was written to teach us, so that through endurance and the encouragement of the Scriptures we might have hope (Romans 15:4).

Snack Attack

Mealtime Prayer:

"Lord, help me to remember that Your timing is perfect. Amen."

Appetizer:

Did you know the word *cookie* actually comes from the Dutch word *koekje*, pronounced "kook-ya," which means "little cake"? Why do you think they gave it this name?

Main Course:

Have you ever sneaked a treat before dinner? Your stomach is growling. Your patience is wearing out. You munch a cookie (or two or three) just to ease your hunger. What happens when dinnertime arrives? What if you were served your favorite meal, and you were too full to enjoy it? How would you feel? What are the benefits (and hard parts) about waiting?

Table Talk:

- How is eating snacks before dinner like filling your life up with what you think is best?
- What are some things you want to "fill up on" that God might tell you "Don't eat" or "Wait"?
- Why is God's timing and His "food" best?
- How can you remind yourself to wait for God's best?
- Write out the word *koekje* on a piece of paper. Underneath it, write out five things that you will trust God and wait for.

Vitamins and Minerals:

Be still before the LORD and wait patiently for him (Psalm 37:7).

What's on Your Label?

Mealtime Prayer:

"Dear Lord, a name isn't something I can see or taste or touch. But help me to remember that it sticks with me wherever I go. Amen."

Appetizer:

Grab three cans of food from the cupboard. What things on the label make customers want to buy them? If your mom and dad were cans in a supermarket, what good things would you put on their labels? "Hard worker"? "Good cook"? "Generous neighbor"? What labels would go on a can with your name?

Main Course:

If you had to choose between eating "Slimy Green-Grass Pudding" and "Chocolate Delight," which would you choose? How would the name influence your decision?

How are people also labeled by their actions? What labels do we give others? What label do your friends or family know you by?

Read 1 Samuel 18:30. What does it say about David? David's name is still known to this day. People around the world know about King David. What good things is David remembered for?

Table Talk:

- How will others treat you if your name is respected? What if your name isn't respected?
- What can you do to make sure you have a good name? (Read Proverbs 3:3–4.)

Vitamins and Minerals:

A good name is more desirable than great riches (Proverbs 22:1).

The Great Provider

Mealtime Prayer:
One purpose of prayer is to tell God how wonderful He is. Pray this prayer:
"God is great. God is good. We will thank Him for this food. By His hand, must all be fed. Thanks be to God for daily bread. Amen."

Appetizer:
Ever had a picnic at the beach when sand got into your food? The skeletons of many Egyptians show teeth that were worn down from eating sandy bread.[1] Any guesses why? Too many picnics? In the days when pharaohs ruled Egypt, bread was made from grain called emmer wheat. As the wheat was ground, small bits of sand often got mixed in.[2]

Main Course:
Read Genesis 41:33–41, 48–49, 53–57. How did God help Joseph? How did Joseph help Pharaoh? How was Joseph rewarded? Who should get the praise, God or Joseph? Why?

Table Talk:

- How many things did God provide in this story? What were they? (Hint: not just food.)
- What has God provided for you?
- How are you rewarded when you listen to God?
- How are the people around you rewarded?

Vitamins and Minerals:
[God] provides food for those who fear him (Psalm 111:5).

---

1. Russell T. Reynolds, "Mummy's Teeth," Egyptology, Doc Reynolds, 2005, http://www.docreynolds.com/egyptology/pages/b_ramesesIxray_png.htm.
2. G. F. Stallknecht, K. M. Gilbertson, and J. F. Ranney, "Alternative Wheat Cereals as Food Grains: Einkorn, Emmer, Spelt, Kamut, and Triticale," Horticulture, Purdue University, 1996, http://www.hort.purdue.edu/newcrop/proceedings1996/v3-156.html#EMMEROrigin.

It's Good for You!

Mealtime Prayer:

Thank the Lord that He has given you food to make your body strong and His Word to make your spirit strong.

Appetizer:

Did you know that broccoli has been served up for dinner for at least 2,000 years? (Parts of the Bible have been around even longer!)[1]

If you could outlaw one vegetable, what would it be?

Main Course:

Have you ever heard your mom say, "Eat your broccoli; it's good for you"? Believe it or not, your parents put broccoli (or other veggies) on your plate because they love you. What good things are in broccoli? How is the Bible like broccoli? What good things are in the Bible?

Of course, the best part is that the Bible doesn't taste like mush or leave little green things between your teeth! What does the Bible leave you with instead?

Table Talk:

- How does eating nutritious foods like broccoli make you feel?
- How does reading the Bible make you feel? Just reading it is not enough. What else do you need to do?

Vitamins and Minerals:

[Moses] took the Book of the Covenant and read it to the people. They responded, "We will do everything the LORD has said; we will obey" (Exodus 24:7).

---

1. "Cabbage Flowers for Food," Aggie Horticulture, Texas AgriLife Extension Service, http://aggie-horticulture.tamu.edu/archives/parsons/publications/vegetabletravelers/broccoli.html.

God-Sized Water Bottle

Mealtime Prayer:

Pray Psalm 42:1:

> *"As the deer pants for streams of water, so my soul pants for you, O God."*

Appetizer:

Did you know that in many places, about 6,800 gallons of water are required to grow a day's food for a family of four?[1] What other things is water used for?

Main Course:

Have you ever shared a water bottle on a hot day? Did you get to take as much as you wanted? Why or why not?

It's not like that with God. God is available anytime to give you all the spiritual water you need. If you could find a water bottle big enough for that, what would it be like?

What things are true of both Jesus and water?

Table Talk:

- Can you pray so often that God doesn't have time for anyone else? Does God ever have to limit His time with you? Why or why not?
- If for one day your parents had no limits on what you could do, how would you want to spend the day?
- God has no limits. How can you spend your days with God?

Vitamins and Minerals:

[Jesus said,] "Whoever believes in me . . . streams of living water will flow from him" (John 7:38).

---

1. "Water Footprint Q&A," Siemens, 2011, http://www.water.siemens.com/en/about_us/Pages/Water_Footprint.aspx.

150 Watts

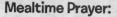

Mealtime Prayer:
Along with thanking God for your food, thank Him for being the Light of the World. Ask God to let His light shine through you.

Appetizer:
Have someone volunteer to be blindfolded and then walk around the table. Be careful the volunteer doesn't get hurt! Have him or her take the blindfold off and walk around again. What differences are there between being able to see and being blindfolded?

Main Course:
If you were in a strange room in the dark, how would you walk around in it? What dangers might be hidden in the dark?

Some people are afraid of the dark. What could their reasons be?

The Bible says the world is full of darkness because of sin. How is sin like darkness? How can it be dangerous? How does sin keep us from going the right way?

Table Talk:
- The Bible says that Jesus is the Light of the World. What does that mean?
- How can being a Christian help you to see more clearly?
- How can following Jesus keep you from danger?
- How can following Jesus make you a light?

Vitamins and Minerals:
[Jesus said,] "I am the light of the world. Whoever follows me will never walk in darkness, but will have the light of life" (John 8:12).

Name That Tune

Mealtime Prayer:
Use Psalm 150:1–2 as your prayer:

> *"Praise the LORD. Praise God in his sanctuary; praise him in his mighty heavens. Praise him for his acts of power; praise him for his surpassing greatness. Amen."*

Appetizer:
Play Name That Tune. Have someone hum a song while the others try to guess the name of the song. Keep playing until everyone has had a turn to hum a song.

Main Course:
What do you enjoy about music? Why do you think there are so many different styles of music? What kind do you like the best? Why would God create us with the ability to sing and play musical instruments?

The book of Psalms is a collection of songs, poems, and praises. Many of the psalms were written to be sung to the music of stringed instruments. Name three types of stringed instruments. How can songs be used for praise and worship?

Table Talk:
- Music is powerful. Does God care about the kind of music we listen to? Why? How does music affect you?
- Make up words of praise to the tune of your favorite song, to "Jingle Bells," and to "Mary Had a Little Lamb."

Vitamins and Minerals:
I will sing to the LORD all my life; I will sing praise to my God as long as I live (Psalm 104:33).

Blowin' in the Wind

Mealtime Prayer:
Thank God for the many ways He shows Himself to us and for the wonders of His creation.

Appetizer:
Have everyone go outside or look out a window. Is the wind blowing? How do you know? Can you see it? How do you know when wind is there?

Main Course:
What would you say to someone who said there was no such thing as wind? How would you prove there was? How is God like the wind? How can we hear God? What does God do that lets us know He exists?

Table Talk:
- Romans 1:20 says, "For since the creation of the world God's invisible qualities—his eternal power and divine nature—have been clearly seen, being understood from what has been made, so that men are without excuse." How can we see God in nature?
- What other things show you God is real?
- What would you say to someone who says you can't prove there is a God?

Vitamins and Minerals:
The heavens declare the glory of God; the skies proclaim the work of his hands (Psalm 19:1).

Eat Your Veggies

Mealtime Prayer:

Thank God that His Word teaches us right from wrong. Ask Him to help you choose what is right.

Appetizer:

The word *vegetable* contains the word *table*. What vegetables are on your table? If you had to eat only vegetables, what would you choose for breakfast? If you could be any kind of vegetable, what kind would you be? Why?

Main Course:

Daniel was a young man who loved the Lord. He was invited to a royal feast, but there was a problem. Daniel didn't want to eat the meat because he knew it had been offered to an idol. He decided to eat vegetables instead.

Read what happened in Daniel 1:8–17. How did God honor Daniel for making the right choice?

Table Talk:

- Think of times when you chose not to do something wrong. What happened?
- How can you know what is right when you face a tough choice?
- How can your conscience and/or the Bible help you know the difference?

Vitamins and Minerals:

Love must be sincere. Hate what is evil; cling to what is good (Romans 12:9).

Good News!

Mealtime Prayer:
Thank God for the good news, which gives "spiritual food" for our souls.

Appetizer:
Time for a good-news session. Have everyone take a turn to share some good news from today or this past week. Next, have someone get a newspaper. Read some of the headlines. Does the newspaper tell good news, bad news, or both?

Main Course:
What are the first four books in the New Testament called? (The Gospels: Matthew, Mark, Luke, and John.) *Gospel* means "good news." What is that good news? (The story of Jesus and how He came to the world to bring salvation to all people.) Why is this good news? What other good news does the Bible tell?

Table Talk:
- Why would you rather hear good news than bad?
- How does the good news of salvation change how you act?
- Name three things you can do with the good news from the Gospels.

Vitamins and Minerals:
But these [words] are written that you may believe that Jesus is the Christ, the Son of God, and that by believing you may have life in his name (John 20:31).

Fish Dinner

Mealtime Prayer:

Sing the prayer today to the tune of "Row, Row, Row Your Boat."

> *"Bless, bless, bless this food, Bless all present here. Help us now to spread Your love to people far and near."*

Appetizer:

The largest animal ever is a blue whale, measuring up to 110 feet. That's like 29 kids lying in a straight line! The heart of a blue whale weighs as much as a car.[1] What's the biggest fish you've ever seen?

Main Course:

Read Jonah 1:1–2; 1:17–2:10. Why did God send Jonah to Nineveh? How did God get Jonah back on track? Do you think Jonah will ever forget that fish's dinner?

Looking at what happened when Jonah preached to the Ninevites (Jonah 3:10), why was it so important for him to go to Nineveh?

Table Talk:

- If you rode in a fish's belly, would you get seasick? What do you think it would be like?
- How might you be like Jonah? What important job could God have for you to do?
- Why should you obey God? What reminds you or helps you to do that?

Vitamins and Minerals:

Remind the people to be subject to rulers and authorities, to be obedient, to be ready to do whatever is good (Titus 3:1).

---

1. "Blue Whale," Animals, *National Geographic*, http://animals.nationalgeographic.com/animals/mammals/blue-whale/.

Got Milk?

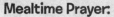

Mealtime Prayer:
Pray the words from Psalm 145:15–16. (Have the leader read the first line, then the rest read the next line together.)

> *Leader: "The eyes of all look to you."*
> *Response: "And you give them their food at the proper time."*
> *Leader: "You open your hand."*
> *Response: "And satisfy the desires of every living thing."*

Appetizer:
Did you know that cows are good for more than milk and steaks? What else comes from cows? (Basketballs are made from cowhides. Crayons come from cow fat![1])

Main Course:
Follow the milk on your table backward to see where it comes from. Your parents may buy milk at the store, but how does it get there? Where do delivery drivers get it? How does the dairy get it out of the cows? What do cows need to produce milk? Who made the grass that cows eat? Who made the sunshine and rain that makes the grass grow? God is responsible for the milk in your glass. The same is true for every other food. God is the ultimate Provider!

Table Talk:
- What else ultimately comes from God?
- Follow some other things backward. Where did your T-shirt come from? What about your stereo or TV?
- How do things like friendship, happiness, and safety lead back to God?

Vitamins and Minerals:
[God] has shown kindness by giving you rain from heaven and crops in their seasons; he provides you with plenty of food and fills your hearts with joy (Acts 14:17).

---

1. "Other Daisy Products," Oracle ThinkQuest, http://library.thinkquest.org/03oct/01272/id39.htm.

Gifts That Money Can't Buy

Mealtime Prayer:
Ask the Lord to help you find ways to give to people in need, not just to those who can pay you back.

Appetizer:
Did you know that for $299 you could buy your mom a hand-painted vase from Sweden? Or for $350 you could buy your dad a gold belt buckle? What could your parents buy for you with that much money? What gifts can money not buy?

Main Course:
Read Luke 10:30–34. What do you think loving others and giving to others mean to Jesus? What is the greatest gift in this story?

Look at the people sitting around the table. Think of a gift you could give each person without leaving the room. Now give it.

Table Talk:
- What is a gift that you really appreciated? Why? Who gave it to you?
- What did the Samaritan expect to get back from the man he helped? Why does God ask us to give without expecting anything back?
- Who is one person you might label an enemy? What's one thing you could give to him or her?

Vitamins and Minerals:
[Jesus said,] "But love your enemies, do good to them, and lend to them without expecting to get anything back" (Luke 6:35).

Heard WHAT on the Grapevine?

Mealtime Prayer:

> *"Lord, just as I'm careful about what goes into my mouth,*
> *help me to be careful about what comes out of my mouth. Amen."*

Appetizer:

Place the handle of your fork between your upper lip and your nose. Try holding it there (no hands!) while saying this tongue twister: "Delicious desserts are dandy after dinner."

Main Course:

Play a game of Grapevine. Whisper one of the following sentences into the ear of the person to your right—say it only once. That person has to repeat the sentence to the next person. Continue until the sentence travels around the table. The last person says the sentence aloud. How close was the sentence at the end to the sentence in the beginning?

Sentences:

1. Purple pretzels are the biggest craze among the people of Afghanistan.
2. I don't like popcorn; I like crackers, and my friend Sue likes cheddar cheese.
3. Corn, peas, and milk make an awful drink when they are mixed together.

Table Talk:

- Why don't the sentences end the same as they start?
- What happens to gossip when you share it with other people? Why?
- What kinds of things does gossip lead to?
- How can you stop gossip before it starts? When you hear it?

Vitamins and Minerals:

Whoever spreads slander is a fool (Proverbs 10:18).

King on the Mountain

Mealtime Prayer:

As you thank God for your food, thank Him for the Bible, which teaches you how to live. Ask Him to help you obey His commands.

Appetizer:

As a family, make up 10 new rules for your house. They can be serious or funny. Put them in order of importance from 1 to 10.

Main Course:

After Moses led the Israelites across the Red Sea, they traveled through the wilderness and camped by a big mountain. Moses climbed up the mountain to talk to God. God gave Moses 10 laws to tell the people. One day God wrote those rules on two tablets of stone and gave them to Moses. These rules are known as the Ten Commandments. How many can you name? (See Exodus 20.)

Why did God make rules? Why do some people not like rules?

Table Talk:

- The first four commandments are about how we relate to God. Why do you think God put those first?
- Why do you think the commandment to honor your parents is right in the middle?
- Why does God want you to obey His commandments?
- What happens when you obey God's commandments?

Vitamins and Minerals:

[Jesus said,] "If you love me, you will obey what I command" (John 14:15).

A Rocky Ride

Mealtime Prayer:

Have someone pray the following prayer:
"Dear Lord Jesus, God's only Son,
To You we lift our praise.
Fill our hearts with peace and love,
And bless us all our days. Amen "

Appetizer:

Who are you? Have each person say his or her full name and describe himself
or herself with one description. (For example, "My name is James John Jones,
and I am tall.")

How do you know who people really are?

Main Course:

When Jesus was living on the earth, many people saw Him do amazing things
and often wondered who He really was. Read the story about Jesus calming the
storm in Matthew 8:23–27.

How would you have felt if you were in the boat during the storm? What
would you have thought after Jesus calmed the storm? Why did Jesus have the
power to calm the storm?

Table Talk:

- Who is Jesus? How do you know?
- What would you say to someone who says, "Jesus was just a good
  person"?
- Why is it important that Jesus is God? How does it help you in
  difficult times?

Vitamins and Minerals:

Simon Peter answered, "You are the Christ, the Son of the living God"
(Matthew 16:16).

Construction Zone

Mealtime Prayer:
Thank God that He is in charge. Ask Him to help you listen to Him and live the way He wants.

Appetizer:
Guess how many different languages there are today. (Answer: more than 6,800)[1] How many can you speak? What would happen if everyone in your family spoke a different language?

Main Course:
After the flood, God told Noah's family, "Be fruitful and increase in number and fill the earth" (Genesis 9:1). Why do you think God said that?

Soon there were many more people, but they wanted to stay together instead of filling the earth. They built a city and a tall tower that they hoped would reach to heaven. Why did God not want them to do this?

God made them speak in different languages. How did that force the people to stop building, to separate, and to spread out as God wanted them to?

Table Talk:
- Do you think people from the same family still spoke the same language after God gave new languages? Why or why not?
- What was the main thing those people did wrong?
- What happens when you do things your way instead of God's way?

Vitamins and Minerals:
[The LORD declares,] "My word . . . will not return to me empty, but will accomplish what I desire and achieve the purpose for which I sent it" (Isaiah 55:11).

---

1. Stephen R. Anderson, "How Many Languages Are There in the World?" Linguistics Society of America, May 2004, http://www.lsadc.org/info/pdf_files/howmany.pdf; "How Many Languages Are There?" Discovery Channel, 2011, http://curiosity.discovery.com/question/how-many-languages-are-there.

What Time Is It?

Mealtime Prayer:
Have someone read the following prayer:
> *"Lord, we thank You for our meal,*
> *For times to laugh and times to heal,*
> *For times to work and times to rest.*
> *Show us, Lord, which way is best. Amen."*

Appetizer:
Have each person tell which of the four seasons he or she likes best and why.

Main Course:
What are some activities that occur in each season? Seasons also occur in our lives, such as a time for playing sports or a season for studying hard. Why are there times when we laugh and times when we cry? At what times should we speak, and when should we be silent? Why did God create a time for everything?

Table Talk:
- Why is it hard to trust that God's timing is perfect?
- Name two things you're waiting to see happen. What helps you wait patiently?
- How does God know what you need? How does God know your thoughts and feelings?

Vitamins and Minerals:
There is a time for everything, and a season for every activity under heaven (Ecclesiastes 3:1).

The Real Big Shot

Mealtime Prayer:

"O Lord, You are greater than everything and everyone in heaven and on earth."

Appetizer:

Did you know that Andruw Jones of the Atlanta Braves was the youngest player to ever hit a home run in the World Series? He was only 19.[1] If you could break a world record, what would it be?

Main Course:

Who are your heroes? To the world, these people are big shots, but men and women of the Bible knew who was responsible for success.

Read Genesis 45:8. Who really made Joseph ruler of all Egypt?

Read Esther 4:12–14. Why was Esther placed in the palace?

Read 1 Timothy 2:3–7. Why was Paul raised up as a teacher?

It's fine to appreciate talents and to respect people who have been especially blessed. But why should we be careful of thinking too highly of others? To God, are some people more important than others? Why or why not?

Table Talk:

- Name three people you think are more important than you are. Are they really?
- Who is the only true big shot?
- Why is it good to let others know who helps you succeed and gives you your talents?

Vitamins and Minerals:

Many are the plans in a man's heart, but it is the LORD's purpose that prevails (Proverbs 19:21).

---

1. 1996 World Series, *Baseball Almanac*, http://www.baseball-almanac.com/ws/yr1996ws.shtml.

When Less Is More

Mealtime Prayer:

Ask God to show you ways you can give to others what matters to you.

Appetizer:

Fill a small cup with warm water. Put a couple tablespoons of a favorite drink in a large cup. (Make sure the cups aren't see-through.) Hold up the cups so everyone can see how full they are. Ask which cup they'd rather have. After they choose, show them the inside of the cups. Why did they choose the one they did? How did they feel when they first saw the amounts? Which tasted better?

Main Course:

What matters more, amount or content? What would mean more: if a person with a truckload of cookies offered you one cookie, or if a friend who had only one cookie gave it to you? Why?

A similar thing happened in the Bible. Read Mark 12:41–44.

Table Talk:

- Why were the widow's coins worth more than what the others gave? Why do you think she gave it all?
- If you gave your last coins away like she did, how would you survive?
- What stops you from giving sometimes?
- What can you give today? Who can you give it to?

Vitamins and Minerals:

[Jesus said,] "They all gave out of their wealth; but she, out of her poverty, put in everything—all she had to live on" (Mark 12:44).

Not Hanging with the Crowd

Mealtime Prayer:
Sing a verse of "I Have Decided to Follow Jesus":
> *"Though none go with me, still I will follow.* [Sing three times.]
> *No turning back, no turning back."*

Appetizer:
What is the most unusual food you can think of? What is the most unusual animal? Have you ever felt unusual or out of place? For example, have you been the only kid at the lunch table eating carrot sticks while everyone else is chomping on snack cakes? Why can it be hard being unusual?

Main Course:
In what ways does God call us to be different? Moses was a Hebrew baby adopted by Pharaoh's daughter. He could have spent his days living in riches, but what did he do instead? (Read Hebrews 11:23–25.)

When God asked Moses to take the Hebrews out of Egypt, Moses was nervous. Did he let his nervousness about being different stop him? (Read Exodus 5:1.)

Hebrews 11:27 says, "[Moses] persevered because he saw him who is invisible." Who is that invisible person?

Table Talk:
- When is one time you were forced to be different? How did you feel? How did God help you?
- What can be really good about being different? What are three things that make you different that you can be thankful for?

Vitamins and Minerals:
This is what the LORD Almighty, the God of Israel, says, ". . . Obey me, and I will be your God and you will be my people. Walk in all the ways I command you, that it may go well with you" (Jeremiah 7:21, 23).

No More Baby Food!

Mealtime Prayer:
Ask the Lord to help you crave His Word as much as you crave food for your body.

Appetizer:
Hide your family's meal, and instead serve milk, crackers, and applesauce. Note your family's reaction. Ask them, "Would you be satisfied with this meal? Why or why not? Would you want to eat this meal every day?" Bring out the real meal and talk about the difference between the two.

Main Course:
Read Hebrews 5:11–14. When it comes to God's Word, why are some people content with "baby food" beliefs? Why are "baby food" beliefs easier to handle and "digest"? What is "solid food" for Christians? How do you think God-followers can move on to solid food? What do you have to be aware of to move on to "solid food"? (The difference between good and evil.)

Table Talk:
- What would you be like if you only ate baby food?
- How will studying the Bible help you "grow up" in your faith?
- What is one thing that you know is evil? What is one thing that is good? How did you know the difference?

Vitamins and Minerals:
But solid food is for the mature, who by constant use have trained themselves to distinguish good from evil (Hebrews 5:14).

Who Said It?

Mealtime Prayer:

Thank God for the messages He gives us in the Bible and for His messengers.

Appetizer:

Let's play some Who Said It? Bible trivia:

Q: Who told Pharaoh there was going to be a famine in Egypt? (Answer: Joseph)

Q: Who was sent to preach God's Word to the people of Nineveh? (Answer: Jonah)

Q: Who told Mary she was going to have a baby who would be the Messiah? (Answer: The angel Gabriel)

Main Course:

Have you ever had to deliver a message? Who was the message for? What was it? Why was it important to get the message right?

In the Bible, God often used messengers to deliver messages for Him. How many can you think of? Sometimes He used people, sometimes He used angels, and one time He even used a donkey! What are some messages you've read in the Bible? How are they useful for you today?

Table Talk:

- What should you do with God's message? If you were to send a reply, what would it say?
- What or who are some of God's messengers today?
- Name three messages from God that you can give to others.

Vitamins and Minerals:

[Jesus said,] "For I did not speak of my own accord, but the Father who sent me commanded me what to say and how to say it" (John 12:49).

Truth or Consequences

Mealtime Prayer:
Have someone say the following prayer:
> *"Lord, we thank You for Your Word,*
> *We know Your Word is true.*
> *Help us to obey Your Word in everything we do.*
> *Amen."*

Appetizer:
Play a game of Truth or Consequences. Divide the family into two teams. Have each team make up five true-or-false questions about anything you can think of. Have the teams take turns asking the questions. The team that gets the most correct answers wins. The other team has to do the dishes!

Main Course:
Think of some of the excuses you have heard. What was the strangest excuse you've heard that was true? How did you know it was true?

Think of some lies you've heard or told. How was it discovered that they were lies? What happened?

Table Talk:
- What is the difference between the consequences of telling the truth and telling lies?
- Why is truth the best policy?
- Where or when is it hard for you to tell the truth? What can help you be honest?

Vitamins and Minerals:
A false witness will not go unpunished, and he who pours out lies will not go free (Proverbs 19:5).

It's a Boy!

Mealtime Prayer:

Think of a time when God answered a specific prayer. Thank Him for answering your prayers.

Appetizer:

Have each person say his or her full name and tell its meaning. If you don't know what your name means, look it up online. Does the meaning of your name describe who you are as a person? Why or why not?

Main Course:

Have you ever wanted something so badly that it was all you could think about? What was it? Did you get it?

There was a woman in the Bible named Hannah who didn't have any children. She wanted a son so badly that it was all she could think about. Every day she prayed for a son until God finally answered her prayer. Hannah named her baby boy Samuel, which means "heard of God." Why do you think God answered Hannah's prayer? Why do you think Hannah named her baby Samuel?

Table Talk:

- Is it okay to ask God for something you really, really want? Why or why not?
- What's more important—telling God what you want or getting what you want? Why?
- What should you do if you don't get what you ask for?
- Why does God want you to pray?

Vitamins and Minerals:

Pray continually; give thanks in all circumstances, for this is God's will for you in Christ Jesus (1 Thessalonians 5:17–18).

Back to the Cradle

Mealtime Prayer:
Thank God for sending His Son to earth to save us from our sins.

Appetizer:
Get out family baby pictures ahead of time, and bring them to the table.
Ask these questions:
Q: When were you born?
Q: Where were you born?
Q: What did you weigh at birth?

Main Course:
Tell each child one special thing about when he or she
was a baby. Why are babies so special? Why do they need
to be cared for? What would happen if babies didn't grow up?

There was a man in the Bible named Nicodemus who spoke to Jesus one
night. Jesus told Nicodemus that he had to be born again to see the kingdom
of God. Nicodemus was very confused. He thought he had to become a baby
again (John 3:1–6). What did Jesus mean?

Table Talk:
- How is becoming a Christian like being a baby?
- How can new Christians grow spiritually?
- When do Christians stop growing? When should they stop?
- How old are you spiritually? Compare that to your physical age.
  What would you be? A newborn? A toddler? A teenager? Why?

Vitamins and Minerals:
[Jesus answered,] "I tell you the truth, no one can see the kingdom of God
unless he is born again" (John 3:3).

Be a Peach

Mealtime Prayer:

"Heavenly Father up above,
Fill us with Your peace and love.
Help us to be kind and good
and do the things we know we should.
Thank You for our food today.
Hear us, Father, as we pray. Amen."

Appetizer:

Gather as many different kinds of fruit as you can, and place them on the table. For each type of fruit, think of positive character traits that begin with the same letter (for example, peach: pleasant, polite).

Main Course:

If you could be any kind of fruit tree, what would you be? Why?

The Bible says that Christians are like trees that bear fruit. The "fruit" we bear, however, isn't the fruit we eat, like apples or bananas. God's Spirit in us helps us bear His fruit. The fruit is seen in the way we act and how we treat others. What kinds of God's "fruit" are growing in your house?

Table Talk:

- What kinds of "fruit" do you want to grow on your "tree"? How can you help it grow?
- Why does God care about how you act and treat other people?
- What kind of care would help your "tree" produce good fruit?

Vitamins and Minerals:

But the fruit of the Spirit is love, joy, peace, patience, kindness, goodness, faithfulness, gentleness and self-control. Against such things there is no law (Galatians 5:22–23).

I Spy!

Mealtime Prayer:
Think about some of the wonderful things that God has created for you to enjoy every day. Thank Him for those things when you pray.

Appetizer:
Count how many living things (bigger than your thumbnail) are in your house, including plants and pets. Guess how many different kinds of trees and animals there are in the world. (Answer: There are more than 23,000 kinds of trees,[1] and over two million kinds of animals![2])

Main Course:
Look at the food on your plate and the items on the table. Look at the floor, the ceiling, and everything in between. Look at the people sitting around the table. Look out a window or walk outside. Ready? Now take turns sharing one thing you noticed that is a part of God's creation, and tell how it's good for you. (For example, water is healthy for our bodies and helps plants and trees to grow.) Keep taking turns until everyone shares what he or she has found.

Table Talk:
- Why do you think God created so many different things? What could the purpose of each one be?
- How should we care for all the things God made?

Vitamins and Minerals:
God saw all that he had made, and it was very good (Genesis 1:31).

---

1. "Tree Facts," North Carolina State University, http://www.ncsu.edu/project/treesofstrength/treefact.htm.
2. Andrea Thompson, "Greatest Mysteries: How Many Species Exist on Earth?" Live Science, August 3, 2007, http://www.livescience.com/4593-greatest-mysteries-species-exist-earth.html.

Be a Wise Guy

Mealtime Prayer:
As you thank God for His blessings, ask Him to bless you with the gift of wisdom.

Appetizer:
Read Proverbs 1:8, and then make up a proverb together as a family. (For example, he who eats vegetables gets dessert.)

Main Course:
If you could have anything in the world, what would you ask for and why? God told King Solomon he could have anything he wanted. Do you know what Solomon asked for? (He asked for wisdom.) Why do you think King Solomon asked for that? The Bible tells us that King Solomon was wiser than any other man (see 1 Kings 4:31). How could wisdom be helpful to a king? How can wisdom help you?

Table Talk:
- Name some situations in which you could use wisdom. (For example, when a classmate asks you to give the answer for a test question.)
- How can you get wisdom?
- Just having wisdom isn't enough. You have to use it. What would you do with your wisdom when you got it? (For example, would you say no, tell the teacher, or pray for your classmate?)

Vitamins and Minerals:
If any of you lacks wisdom, he should ask God, who gives generously to all without finding fault, and it will be given to him (James 1:5).

Salt of the Earth

Mealtime Prayer:

Sing the prayer below to the tune "Zip-a-Dee-Doo-Dah":

"Zip-a-dee-doo-dah, zip-a-dee-ay,
We are grateful for Your blessing today.
Here at God's table, love's everywhere.
Let us be salt, with good things to share!"

Appetizer:

Did you know that Roman soldiers were given a salt allowance, or salarium? Salt was valuable like money. This is where the word *salary* comes from. What kind of salary would you work for if money were no longer the way people got paid?

Main Course:

Salt has military importance. Thousands of Napoleon's troops died when their wounds would not heal because of a lack of salt. Also, in 1777, during the Revolutionary War, the British Lord Howe was jubilant when he succeeded in capturing General Washington's salt supply.[1]

Salt is important today. It keeps our bodies balanced and our blood stable. It preserves food and adds flavor. It also makes us thirsty. One handful of salt goes a long way.

Table Talk:

- Jesus called His believers "the salt of the earth." How are Christians like salt? How do we bring stability? Preserve goodness? Add flavor?
- How do believers help others thirst for God? How does a handful of Christ followers go a long way?
- Name one way you can be "salt" to those around you today.

Vitamins and Minerals:

[Jesus said,] "You are the salt of the earth" (Matthew 5:13).

---

1. "History of Salt," Salt Works, http://www.saltworks.us/salt_info/si_HistoryOfSalt.asp.

A New PB&J

Mealtime Prayer:
Look around the table at all the good things God has provided. Praise the Lord for those things.

Appetizer:
Read Psalm 148:1–5. Give each family member a special word or phrase to shout, such as "Amen," "I believe," or "Joy," every time you read the word *praise*. If you like, have each one lift his or her hands while shouting.

Main Course:
Have you ever had one of those difficult days when nothing seems to go right? Try a PB&J. Not a peanut butter and jelly sandwich but *praise*, *belief*, and *joy*. Name three ways these three things can change your day.

Table Talk:
- What things has God done that you can praise Him for? (For example, He made it possible to have ice cream.) Why does God deserve to be praised?
- What things has God put in your life that give you joy? How does a relationship with God bring joy?

Vitamins and Minerals:
I will praise you as long as I live, and in your name I will lift up my hands (Psalm 63:4).

Don't Go Solo

Mealtime Prayer:

Thank God for each person at your table. Ask Him to show you ways to work together as a team.

Appetizer:

Look around. What work needs to be done around your house tonight? Does the kitchen need to be cleaned? Does the yard need to be raked? How can these chores become fun? After the meal, instead of "going solo," pick one chore to tackle as a team. Pay attention to how quickly the work gets done, and make it fun (for example, by trying to finish in the time it takes to sing a song).

Main Course:

What does *solo* mean? Even though Jesus was all-powerful, He didn't go solo. He called 12 men to help Him in His work and called them His disciples. What did Jesus do for His disciples? How did those disciples help Jesus?

Those men, and all the believers who followed Jesus, were part of God's plan.

No going solo in God's kingdom!

Table Talk:

- What are some ways you can be part of God's team?
- Jesus prayed, "Holy Father, protect them . . . so that they may be one as we are one" (John 17:11). What does that mean? How can you be one (be close and at peace) with other people?
- What kinds of things keep you from being one with others?

Vitamins and Minerals:

Two are better than one, because they have a good return for their work (Ecclesiastes 4:9).

Gigantic Grocery List

Mealtime Prayer:

"Thank You, O Lord, for this food. May we always have faith that You will provide. Amen."

Appetizer:

Did you know that in one year an average zoo elephant eats 1,600 loaves of bread, 2,000 potatoes, 1,500 gallons of mixed grains, 100,000 pounds of hay, 12,000 pounds of dried alfalfa, and 3,000 other vegetables?[1] How long would it take for you to eat that much food (except for the hay!)?

Main Course:

Have you ever helped make a grocery list? What things did it include? Read Genesis 6:17–22. What do you think Noah's grocery list looked like for the ark? With God's help, Noah built the ark and gathered food for his family *and* the animals. How does God help your parents gather (buy) food for your zoo . . . uh, family?

Table Talk:

- No one had probably seen rain before the flood, and Noah didn't live near water. What would the neighbors have thought of his boat building? Why do you think Noah kept going?
- How is Noah's obedience an example of faith?
- What if Noah hadn't done all God commanded? What might have happened?

Vitamins and Minerals:

By faith Noah, when warned about things not yet seen, in holy fear built an ark to save his family (Hebrews 11:7).

---

1. Zoobooks, *Elephants* (San Diego: Wildlife Education, 1996).

God's Phone Number

Mealtime Prayer:

Pray the Lord's prayer found in Matthew 6:9–13:

"Our Father in heaven, hallowed be your name, your kingdom come, your will be done on earth as it is in heaven. Give us today our daily bread. Forgive us our debts, as we also have forgiven our debtors. And lead us not into temptation, but deliver us from the evil one. Amen.

Appetizer:

Have one person think of a short message, such as "Eat all your vegetables" or "Baseball is a great sport." Without using words, try to get the others to understand the message.

Main Course:

What are the many ways we can communicate to our friends and relatives?

Which form of communication do you like best? What can you do if you don't know someone's telephone number? How can you get God's "number"? In Jeremiah 33:3, God says, "Call to me and I will answer you."

Table Talk:

- What different ways can you talk to God? What kinds of things should you include in your prayers?
- When can you pray?
- How can God hear more than one prayer at the same time?
- How does God communicate with you?

Vitamins and Minerals:

And pray in the Spirit on all occasions with all kinds of prayers and requests (Ephesians 6:18).

Giant Grapes

Mealtime Prayer:

Have each person give thanks to God for a specific blessing he or she is grateful for.

Appetizer:

Using the word *blessings*, think of one or two blessings that begin with each letter of the alphabet. For example, B = bread, L = liver (liver?) . . .

Main Course:

Moses sent 12 spies into the Promised Land of Canaan to check it out. Joshua and Caleb were excited to see the giant grapes and rich, fertile land. But the other spies were afraid because the people were so big. "We can't attack those people," they said (Numbers 13:31). But Joshua and Caleb said, "If the Lord is pleased with us, he will lead us into that land, a land flowing with milk and honey, and will give it to us" (14:8). Why do you think Joshua and Caleb had a different report from the rest of the spies? If you had been one of the spies, would you have been afraid of the giant people or excited about the giant grapes? Why?

Table Talk:

- What blessings (like peace or confidence) can you enjoy if you trust in God?
- What "giants" do you have in your life? Math? A bully? What are you doing about them?
- What "grapes" (like a best friend) do you have in your life? Thank God for them.

Vitamins and Minerals:

Taste and see that the Lord is good; blessed is the man who takes refuge in him (Psalm 34:8).

Talking Stones

Mealtime Prayer:
Think of times when you've seen or heard about God's power in someone's life. Thank Him for those times.

Appetizer:
Guess how long the Jordan River is. Take a wild guess! (Answer: It's 223 miles long)[1]

Main Course:
After Moses died, Joshua was chosen to lead the Israelites across the Jordan River and into the Promised Land. If you had to lead your family across a river, how would you do it? What would you need? Read the exciting story of how Joshua did it in Joshua 3:14—4:7.

Table Talk:
- Why do you think God told Joshua to set up the memorial?
- Why is it important to remember what God does for us?
- What memorials do you have in your home (for example, a photo album)? What do they remind you of?

Vitamins and Minerals:
[God] did this so that all the peoples of the earth might know that the hand of the LORD is powerful and so that you might always fear the LORD your God (Joshua 4:24).

---

1. "Jordan River," *Encyclopedia Britannica*, 2012, http://www.britannica.com/EBchecked/topic/306217/Jordan-River.

Bite Your Tongue!

Mealtime Prayer:
Ask God to help you speak words that are pleasing to Him and kind to others.

Appetizer:
Did you know that the tongue has more than 10,000 taste buds that are grouped into four categories? The taste buds in the front help you taste sweet flavors. The taste buds on the sides taste sour and salty food. The ones in the back taste bitter flavors.[1] Why is this arrangement good when it comes to licking an ice-cream cone?

Main Course:
What does it feel like to bite your tongue? Have you ever heard the saying "Bite your tongue"? What does that mean? When is it best to "bite your tongues"? What happens if you say something you shouldn't? What should you do if you've said something that hurt someone else?

Table Talk:
- Why is it important for you to control your tongue? Why is it hard?
- Come up with two sayings that can help you learn to control what you say.
- How do words affect others? Why does God care what we say?

Vitamins and Minerals:
Listen, for I have worthy things to say; I open my lips to speak what is right (Proverbs 8:6).

1. "What Are Taste Buds?" *KidsHealth*, September 2010, http://kidshealth.org/kid/talk/qa/taste_buds.html.

All in the Family

Mealtime Prayer:
Thank God for all the members in your family. Thank Him also that you are a part of His family.

Appetizer:
If you gave a party for all of your aunts, uncles, cousins, and grandparents, what would it be like and what would you do?

Main Course:
What does the word *family* mean? What are some of the benefits of being in a family? What are some of the responsibilities? How are the people in your family the same? How are they different?

God's family is like yours in some ways. Who is in it? How does a person become part of God's family? How are the people in God's family the same? How are they different?

Table Talk:
- Why would you want to be part of God's family? What responsibilities or "chores" does it have?
- Why does God want people to join His family?
- How can you help to bring more people into God's family?

Vitamins and Minerals:
Consequently, you are no longer foreigners and aliens, but fellow citizens with God's people and members of God's household (Ephesians 2:19).

Better Than Spinach!

Mealtime Prayer:
> *"Lord, when I am weak, You are strong. Help me to get more out of Your Word than from any physical food. Amen."*

Appetizer:
Care to test your strength? Have a thumb-war contest. Intertwine your fingers with another family member's, thumbs sticking up. The goal is to "pin" your partner's thumb with your own. Start by saying, "One, two, three, four, I declare a thumb war. Begin!" Keep your hands connected but try to pin the other person's thumb.

Main Course:
Did you know that eating tons of spinach won't make you big and strong? (Sorry, Popeye!) Spinach doesn't make your muscles bigger, but it does provide you with iron, calcium, vitamin B, and folic acid. Any idea how these help your body?

What (actually who) can make you truly strong? How does God's love make you confident? His presence? His faithfulness?

To help you remember God's strength, write the following powerful promises on a piece of paper and "digest" (think about) one daily: Psalm 89:21; 119:28; Ephesians 3:16; 2 Thessalonians 2:16–17; 3:3. Watch your spiritual muscles grow!

Table Talk:
- What other powerful promises have you found in God's Word (Proverbs and Psalms have lots)?
- How will these verses strengthen your spiritual muscles?
- Along with reading God's Word, what are other ways to strengthen your spiritual muscles?

Vitamins and Minerals:
Strengthen me according to your word (Psalm 119:28).

What's for Dinner?

Mealtime Prayer:

Sing the following prayer to the tune "Heigh Ho, Heigh Ho":

"We know, we know, from whom all good things flow. We thank Him then, we say amen, we know, we know, we know, we know!"

Appetizer:

If you lived in a different country and asked, "What's for dinner?" you might hear: "Lasagna" (Italy); "Goulash" (Hungary); "Pork and sauerkraut" (Germany); "Borscht" or "Cabbage soup" (Ukraine).

Can you think of others?

Main Course:

Would you be surprised if you asked, "What's for dinner?" and were told, "Rocks, sticks, and grass"?

Why do your parents give you the best they can? Why does God give you the best?

Jesus said, "Which of you, if his son asks for bread, will give him a stone? . . . . If you, then, though you are evil, know how to give good gifts to your children, how much more will your Father in heaven give good gifts to those who ask him!" (Matthew 7:9, 11). What do you have to do to get these good gifts from God?

Table Talk:

- Since your parents love you, will they give you anything you ask for? Why or why not? Will God?
- Name five good things God has given you.

Vitamins and Minerals:

[Jesus said,] "For everyone who asks receives; he who seeks finds; and to him who knocks, the door will be opened" (Matthew 7:8).

Surprise Inspection

Mealtime Prayer:

"For this our daily food,
For our health and happiness,
For our salvation and our future heavenly home,
Give us a thankful heart, O Lord. Amen."

Appetizer:

Surprise inspection! If your parents made a surprise inspection of your room, what would they discover? What would you find if you inspected your parents' room?

Main Course:

How would you feel if this were the day you stood before Jesus? Your parents may inspect your room and closets, but what would Jesus inspect? Would He be pleased by what He'd see? Why or why not?

Since Jesus will say, "Well done, good and faithful servant!" (Matthew 25:21) to those who faithfully follow Him, what would you be willing to do to get this response?

Table Talk:

- If you had to stand before Christ today, what might He say?
- What can you do to make sure that your life pleases God?
- What will be the coolest things about seeing Jesus?

Vitamins and Minerals:

For we must all appear before the judgment seat of Christ, that each one may receive what is due him for the things done while in the body, whether good or bad (2 Corinthians 5:10).

Are You Nuts?

Mealtime Prayer:

"Dear God, thank You for the gift of laughter! Amen."

Appetizer:

Why do squirrels spend so much time in trees?
(Answer: To get away from all the nuts on the ground!)

Main Course:

Match the following four nutty names to the correct question below: A. Cashews
B. Coconuts C. Chestnuts D. Peanuts

1. I am called "brain food" because I have two parts that look like lobes of the brain.
2. I'm the most popular nut in the United States, but I'm not really a nut!
3. You shouldn't touch me on the tree. I belong to the poison ivy family.
4. I sometimes float thousands of miles across the Indian and Pacific Oceans.
   (Answers: 1–C, 2–D, 3–A, 4–B.)

Table Talk:

- Has anyone ever said to you: "Are you nuts?" What do you think it means?
- When do you like to laugh and be silly? Why? How do you feel after laughing?
- How is laughing and being silly good for us?
- Where do you think your sense of humor came from? Why do you think God made laughter?
- Name some of the ways you think you may have seen God's sense of humor in life or nature.

Vitamins and Minerals:

The joy of the Lord is your strength (Nehemiah 8:10).

The Animals Are Hungry

Mealtime Prayer:

"Lord, help us all to do our part to get the work done. Help us all to be faithful as we do our chores and to do the best job we can."

Appetizer:

Imagine that you're Noah's family in the dining room of the ark. What kinds of chores—and how many chores—might Dad assign as you talk at the table?

Main Course:

If you ever feel you have too many chores, consider this: There were just eight people in Noah's family to do *all* the work: take care of thousands of animals, carry their food to their pens, give them fresh water and shovel out their pens, day after day. How do you think they felt when they went to bed at night? Why was it important to do their jobs faithfully? (What would have happened if they hadn't? Yuck!)

Table Talk:

- Imagine a bad day on the ark: it smells awful, you're tired, you're sick, the animals are going crazy, and it's feeding time. What can you do to keep from complaining?
- Which of your chores do you not like doing? Why not? Why is it important to do that chore? How can you make yourself do the best job you can do?

Vitamins and Minerals:

Whatever you do, work at it with all your heart, as working for the Lord, not for men, since you know that you will receive an inheritance from the Lord as a reward. It is the Lord Christ you are serving (Colossians 3:23–24).

Holiday Devotions

BIRTHDAY

It's Original

Mealtime Prayer:
Have each family member thank God for the birthday person when you pray.

Appetizer:
Bible birthday trivia:
> Q: How many birthdays did Methuselah have? (Answer: 969)
> Q: How old was Abraham when Isaac was born? (Answer: 100)
> Q: How old was Jesus when He first taught in the temple? (Answer: 12)
> Q: How many earthly years did Jesus live? (Answer: 33)
> Q: How old are you?

Main Course:
When an artist paints a special painting and decides not to make another one like it, it is called an original. Why is an original so valuable?

You, the birthday person, are special and valuable because you are an original. There is no one else like you in the whole world. For every year you are celebrating, your family members will give reasons why you are special. If you are eight years old, they must think of eight reasons. And by the way—happy birthday!

Table Talk:
- Why did God make only one of you?
- How are you different from the other people in your family?
- How can God use you in a special way?

Vitamins and Minerals:
I praise you because I am fearfully and wonderfully made; your works are wonderful, I know that full well (Psalm 139:14).

NEW YEAR'S DAY

If at First You Don't Succeed

Mealtime Prayer:
Thank God for His love and care. Ask Him to show you His will for the coming year.

Appetizer:
Ask each person to share something he or she wants to do this year.

Main Course:
Happy New Year! At the beginning of each new year, people often make plans. Why do you think they do that?

Did you know that God planned your whole life before you were born? Psalm 139:16 says, "All the days ordained for me were written in your book before one of them came to be." Proverbs 16:3 says, "Commit to the LORD whatever you do, and your plans will succeed." What does it mean to succeed? How can you be successful in life?

Table Talk:
- How can you know God's plans for your life?
- Why are God's plans best?
- What do you think God has planned for you this year?

Vitamins and Minerals:
"For I know the plans I have for you," declares the LORD, "plans to prosper you and not to harm you, plans to give you hope and a future" (Jeremiah 29:11).

VALENTINE'S DAY
Show-and-Tell

Mealtime Prayer:
Thank God for the many people who love you and for those you love. Give examples of how He shows His love to you.

Appetizer:
Have each person tell the other family members one thing he or she loves about each of them.

Main Course:
Valentine's Day is a special day to let others know you love them. What did you do today to show your love for someone? What tells you you're loved? What are other ways you can show your love for others (for example, give breakfast in bed, clean the kitchen)?

Table Talk:
- Why do you think God wants us to love one another?
- How can children show love to their parents? How can parents show love to their children?
- How can we show our love for God?

Vitamins and Minerals:
Dear friends, let us love one another, for love comes from God. Everyone who loves has been born of God and knows God (1 John 4:7).

APRIL FOOL'S DAY

Who's a Fool?

Mealtime Prayer:

As you ask God to bless your food, thank Him for times of fun and laughter.

Appetizer:

In 1957, a British TV station played an April Fool's joke on the whole country! The station aired a program about people in Switzerland who harvested pasta from a "spaghetti tree." It showed workers gathering a "bumper crop" of the noodles. Some people even called the station asking how to grow their own spaghetti tree![1]

Main Course:

What April Fool's tricks did you play today? What tricks were played on you? What is the best April Fool's trick you've ever played on someone else?

April Fool's Day is a day when we can play fun tricks on our friends and family. Why do you think it's called April Fool's Day? What is a fool?

Psalm 14:1 says, "The fool says in his heart, 'There is no God.' " Why is someone who doesn't believe in God a fool? What are some other things that fools don't believe in?

Table Talk:

- How can you keep from being a fool?
- Who do you think is happier, a wise person or a foolish person? Why?
- How do you think God feels about fun? Why?

Vitamins and Minerals:

Our mouths were filled with laughter, our tongues with songs of joy (Psalm 126:2).

---

1. "1957: BBC Fools the Nation," On This Day, BBC, 2008, http://news.bbc.co.uk/onthisday/hi/dates/stories/april/1/newsid_2819000/2819261.stm.

GOOD FRIDAY
Who Took the Sun?

Mealtime Prayer:
After you give thanks for your food, have each person, in his or her own words, thank Jesus for dying on the cross.

Appetizer:
Over 700 years before Jesus was born, the prophet Isaiah predicted that Jesus would be crucified (Isaiah 53:5). How did Isaiah know this would happen? What else was predicted about Jesus? What can you predict about next week? How accurate would you be?

Main Course:
Read the story of the crucifixion of Jesus in Luke 23:33–47, and then read Isaiah 53:3–9. How accurate was Isaiah? Why did God tell Isaiah and other prophets what would happen to Jesus?

Table Talk:
- Why do you think the sun went dark the day Jesus died?
- What would you have thought if you had been one of the soldiers there?
- How is Jesus like the sun?
- If God loves Jesus, why didn't He do something to help Him?

Vitamins and Minerals:
God demonstrates his own love for us in this: While we were still sinners, Christ died for us (Romans 5:8).

EASTER SUNDAY
Sunday Surprise

Mealtime Prayer:
Thank Jesus that because of His death and resurrection
we can have the hope of living forever.

Appetizer:
What have been the most important events in our country
in the past 10 years? In all of history?

Main Course:
Two days after Jesus died, Mary Magdalene and Mary the mother of James
went to Jesus' tomb. How do you think they felt when they saw an angel there
instead of Jesus' body? (Read Matthew 28:5–7.)

The soldiers who were guarding the tomb were paid a lot of money to say
that Jesus' disciples stole His body (Matthew 28:12–13). What really happened
to Jesus' body?

Why do you think the soldiers were paid to lie? If you had been one of the
soldiers, what would you have thought and done?

After Jesus' resurrection (rising from the dead), He appeared to some of
His friends and disciples. What would you have said to Jesus if you had been
there?

Table Talk:
- Why is Jesus' resurrection the most important event in history? How
  is it more important than the events you mentioned earlier?
- What does Jesus' resurrection mean to you?
- Why should we tell others about Jesus' resurrection?

Vitamins and Minerals:
Christ died and returned to life so that he might be the Lord of both the dead
and the living (Romans 14:9).

MOTHER'S DAY
Marvelous Moms

Mealtime Prayer:
Have each person tell Mom why she is marvelous. Follow this activity by having everyone pray for her.

Appetizer:
Marvelous Moms Bible Quiz:

> Q: Who prayed for a son and named him Samuel? (Answer: Hannah)
> Q: Who gave birth to a son at a very old age? (Answer: Sarah)
> Q: Who was the mother of Joseph, Jacob's son? (Answer: Rachel)
> Q: Who was the mother of John the Baptist? (Answer: Elizabeth)
> Q: Who was the mother of Jesus? (Answer: Mary)
> Q: What did the mother skunk say to her children before dinner?
>   (Answer: Let's spray)

Main Course:
Why is a mother important to a family? Name all the things your mother does for you from the time you get up in the morning until the time you go to bed at night. How can you show your appreciation for everything she does?

Table Talk:
- Why do you think God created mothers?
- Why did Jesus need a mother?
- Tell your mom you love her and why.

Vitamins and Minerals:
Charm is deceptive, and beauty is fleeting; but a woman who fears the LORD is to be praised (Proverbs 31:30).

MEMORIAL DAY
Flowers and Flags

Mealtime Prayer:
Thank God for your country, your freedom, and His love.

Appetizer:
The first official Memorial Day in the United States was May 5, 1866, as a time to decorate the graves of those who had died in the American Civil War.[1] Why do you think people wanted to do that?

Main Course:
Do you know people who have served their country by being in the army, navy, air force, or marines? People who are in the armed forces make many sacrifices to keep their country safe. What are some you can think of? Troops may even have to go to war and be willing to die while fighting for their country and for freedom.

Memorial Day is a special holiday to honor men and women who have died during wartime. Families and friends put flowers or flags on the graves. Many cities have parades, and some families celebrate with friends and relatives. How do you celebrate Memorial Day?

Table Talk:
- The Bible tells us of someone who was willing to die so we could be set free from sin. Who was that person?
- How can you celebrate your freedom from sin?
- What would you be willing to die for?

Vitamins and Minerals:
[Jesus said,] "Greater love has no one than this, that he lay down his life for his friends" (John 15:13).

---

1. "Memorial Day History," US Department of Veterans Affairs, Nov. 10, 2009, http://www.va.gov/opa/speceven/memday/history.asp.

FATHER'S DAY
Fabulous Fathers

Mealtime Prayer:

Have each person tell Dad why he is fabulous. Thank God for your father and ask everyone to say a prayer for him.

Appetizer:

Fabulous Father Bible Quiz:

> Q: Who became a father when he was 100 years old? (Answer: Abraham)
> Q: Who gave his son a colorful coat? (Answer: Jacob)
> Q: Who was King Solomon's father? (Answer: David)
> Q: Who was the father of John the Baptist? (Answer: Zechariah)
> Q: What did the colt say to his mother? (Answer: Where's my fodder?)

Main Course:

Why are fathers important to a family? What does your father do for you each day to show that he loves you? How can you show your father that you love him and appreciate all that he does for you? Proverbs 23:22 says, "Listen to your father, who gave you life." What does that mean?

Table Talk:

- How can you bring joy to your father?
- Why is it wise to listen to your dad?
- Why did God create fathers?
- Tell your dad you love him and why.

Vitamins and Minerals:

Children's children are a crown to the aged, and parents are the pride of their children (Proverbs 17:6).

INDEPENDENCE DAY
Let's Party!

Mealtime Prayer:
Thank God for the freedom to worship, and ask Him to bless our country.

Appetizer:
What did one firecracker say to the other firecracker? (Answer: "My pop's bigger than your pop!")

Main Course:
How do you celebrate your country's independence? Why? When the people from England settled in America, they formed individual colonies. Eventually there were 13 colonies along the eastern coast. On July 4, 1776, the leaders of the colonies adopted the Declaration of Independence, which gave them freedom from the British government. This meant they could make their own decisions and worship God the way they wanted. The people were so happy they celebrated with marching bands and the chiming of city bells. Since then, the United States has celebrated July 4th as Independence Day. Today, people in the US celebrate with parades, family picnics, and fireworks.

Table Talk:
- What's your favorite part of the celebration? Why?
- Why is religious freedom important?
- If you were one of the colonial leaders, what would you have included in the Declaration of Independence?

Vitamins and Minerals:
Blessed is the nation whose God is the LORD (Psalm 33:12).

THANKSGIVING DAY
Gobble, Gobble

Mealtime Prayer:
Hold hands while you pray. Take turns praying and telling God what you're grateful for.

Appetizer:
Preserve holiday memories with a Thanksgiving Day journal. Every year record the events of the day, the people with whom you celebrated, and specific blessings you are thankful for. What would you include this year?

Main Course:
If you could invent a holiday to celebrate, what would it be? Why?

In 1620, Pilgrims from England came to America for religious freedom. They faced many hardships, and many died. The American Indians helped the Pilgrims by teaching them how to farm and fish. After the first harvest, the Pilgrims and Indians celebrated with a huge feast—turkey, corn, and pumpkin pie! They thanked God for His goodness throughout the year.

In 1863, President Abraham Lincoln appointed a special day of thanksgiving. In Canada, Thanksgiving is celebrated in October rather than November.

Table Talk:
- If you had been a Pilgrim, what would you have been thankful for?
- What do we have today that the Pilgrims didn't have?
- What do you think you'll be thankful for next year?

Vitamins and Minerals:
Give thanks to the LORD, for he is good. His love endures forever (Psalm 136:1).

No Vacancy

Mealtime Prayer:
Thank God that He keeps all of His promises.

Appetizer:
Where is the most unusual place you have ever spent the night?

Main Course:
The prophet Isaiah wrote that Jesus would be born to a virgin. Micah said Jesus would be born in Bethlehem (Micah 5:2).

Seven hundred years later, an angel told the virgin Mary she would have a baby who would be the Son of God (Luke 1:26–33). Caesar Augustus decided to count all the people under Roman rule. So Mary and her fiancé, Joseph, went to Bethlehem to be counted. When they arrived, the inn was full, so they stayed in a stable where they could rest and keep warm (Luke 2:1–7). How could Micah have known about the Roman count (or census) that would force Mary and Joseph to stay in a place better suited for animals? Try predicting something for the next year. (Write it down, and check it next year.)

Table Talk:
- What does the fulfillment of these prophecies tell you about the Bible?
- If the innkeeper knew Mary was going to be the mother of God's Son, do you think he would have acted differently? Why?
- What's your favorite part of Christmas Eve? What could you do to understand what it was like for Mary and Joseph?

Vitamins and Minerals:
The Lord himself will give you a sign: The virgin will be with child and will give birth to a son, and will call him Immanuel (Isaiah 7:14).

CHRISTMAS DAY
The Best Gift

Mealtime Prayer:
What gifts has God given you? Thank Him for these gifts and the gift of His Son.

Appetizer:
Give a verbal gift to each person at the table by giving him or her a specific compliment.

Main Course:
Imagine being in the stable (probably a cave) with Mary. What would it have been like? What would it have smelled like?

Something exciting happened while Joseph and Mary were resting in the stable in Bethlehem. Read about it in Luke 2:6–11.

Table Talk:
- If you were one of the shepherds, how would you have felt? What would you have done?
- Where can you find Jesus today?
- What gifts can you give Him?
- What should you do with the news of His birth?

Vitamins and Minerals:
But the angel said to [Mary], . . . "You are to give him the name Jesus. He will be great and will be called the Son of the Most High" (Luke 1:30–32).

BOXING DAY

What's in the Box?

Mealtime Prayer:

Thank God for the gifts you received at Christmas this year and ask Him for opportunities to give gifts to others.

Appetizer:

Give everyone an empty box. Have them put a small household item in the box. Then exchange boxes. Try to figure out what's inside by shaking the box. Each person can have three guesses before opening his or her box to see what's really inside.

Main Course:

Have you ever heard of Boxing Day? It's not a day when two people get into a boxing ring and punch each other. Boxing Day refers to gift boxes, and if you live in England, Wales, or parts of Canada, you know what it is.

Today, in Canada, Boxing Day is the biggest shopping day of the year. Store owners slash prices, and eager shoppers search for bargains or begin Christmas shopping for the next year. If people get too greedy, however, it may turn into a real "boxing day" after all!

In days of old, landowners or wealthy people gave gifts of money to servants, tradespeople, and other common people. The gifts became known as Christmas boxes and were given on December 26, the day after Christmas. What would you put in imaginary boxes for a cook, housecleaner, and carpenter?

Table Talk:

- How do you think the people felt when they received their gift boxes?
- What do you think they did with their gifts of money?
- Who could you give gifts to after Christmas?

Vitamins and Minerals:

The Lord Jesus himself said: "It is more blessed to give than to receive" (Acts 20:35).

NEW YEAR'S EVE
Looking Back

Mealtime Prayer:

Read the following prayer:

"Thank You for blessings You give us each day,
For times to work and times to play.
Thank You for blessings of health and cheer,
And all of our blessings throughout the year. Amen."

Appetizer:

Get out a pen and paper for each person. Have everyone make a list of God's blessings, or good gifts, this past year. The first one to get to 10 blessings wins. (Give candy as prizes.)

Main Course:

New Year's Eve is the end of another year. Many families celebrate with parties and stay up until midnight. What do you do on New Year's Eve? Why do you think people celebrate it?

New Year's Eve is also a time to look back over the past year and thank God for His blessings. Proverbs 3:33 says, "[God] blesses the home of the righteous." Proverbs 28:20 says, "A faithful man will be richly blessed." What do you think these verses mean?

Table Talk:

- How do you receive God's blessings?
- Sometimes blessings don't seem like blessings at the time. What difficult things this year can you now see were blessings in disguise?
- What is the best thing that happened to you this past year?

Vitamins and Minerals:

O Lord Almighty, blessed is the man who trusts in you (Psalm 84:12).

Theme
Devotions

Search for Treasure

Mealtime Prayer:

"Lord, thank You for the treasures seated around this table. Amen."

Appetizer:

Blackbeard was one of the most famous pirates of all time. If you could give yourself a pirate name, what would it be? The name of Blackbeard's ship was *Queen Anne's Revenge*. If you had a ship, what would you call her? Why?

Pirate Night:

Prepare a treasure hunt. Hide "treasures" in your house—things like a Bible, a picture of your family, and memory-verse cards. (What other "treasures" can you hide?)

Make a map that will lead to these treasures. Fix a hearty pirate meal, such as stew or meat and potatoes. Dress up your family in scarves, eye patches, and fake moustaches (washable mascara works great.) After the hunt, have your meal, and then read Matthew 6:19–21.

Table Talk:

- What type of treasure do moths and rust destroy?
- What type of treasure do you store up in heaven? How?
- What things that you found during the treasure hunt will last for eternity?

Vitamins and Minerals:

For where your treasure is, there your heart will be also (Matthew 6:21).

Upside-Down Gospel

Mealtime Prayer:
Read the Appetizer first. Then use the prayer below later.
"Lord, help me to follow Your ways, even if they are different from the ones I desire. Amen."

Appetizer:
Tonight, do everything backward. Start with dessert, then eat your meal! Try a few things upside-down, such as using your spoon bottom side up! Say your prayer at the end of the meal.

Backward Night:
Now play a backward/upside-down version of Red Light, Green Light. For this game, the red represents the Lord's blood, and you proceed. On green, you stop. Take turns being the caller.

Christianity is often thought of as a backward and upside-down religion. Read Luke 6:27–30.

Table Talk:
- If someone is mean to you, the world says, "Show who's boss." What does Jesus say? (See verse 27.) How will this affect the mean person?
- If someone hits you or takes your things, the world says, "Fight back." What does Jesus say? (See verse 29.) What difference will this response make?
- The world says, "Protect your stuff—you deserve what you have." What does Jesus say? (See verse 30.) Why can you do this without worry?
- Can you think of any other backward, upside-down examples?

Vitamins and Minerals:
[Jesus said,] "But love your enemies, do good to them, and lend to them without expecting to get anything back. Then your reward will be great, and you will be sons of the Most High, because he is kind to the ungrateful and wicked" (Luke 6:35).

Getting to Know You

Mealtime Prayer:
Thank the Lord for some of your favorite things, such as favorite foods, favorite friends, and so on.

Appetizer:
How well do you know your parents? What are their ages? Their eye colors (without looking!)? Their favorite hobbies?

Family Discovery Night:
Cook a family favorite today. Do you know your family well? As you spend time with one another, you discover likes and dislikes. Give each family member a list of these questions. Try to guess the responses before each person answers. Name your . . .

coolest experience	bravest thing done
favorite holiday	favorite summer activity
special skill or talent	favorite food
favorite Bible story	favorite cartoon
favorite animal	favorite place to talk to God
favorite pastime	favorite month
favorite thing to wear	favorite verse

Table Talk:
- How does listening to each other prove you care?
- How can you get to know Jesus better?
- What are some of God's favorite things? Why?
- What did you learn about Jesus recently that you didn't know before?

Vitamins and Minerals:
[Jesus said,] "Whoever has my commands and obeys them, he is the one who loves me. He who loves me will be loved by my Father, and I too will love him and show myself to him" (John 14:21).

Fortune Promises

Mealtime Prayer:

"Lord, may Your promises strengthen my soul just as food strengthens my body. Amen."

Appetizer:

Did you know that you can order cookies with scriptures inside?[1]

Did you know that chopsticks have been traced back as far as the third century BC? Today, chopsticks are used in Japan, Korea, Vietnam, and China, making them the world's second most popular tool for eating. The most popular? Fingers![2]

Chinese Food:

Make or pick up Chinese food. Don't forget the chopsticks and green tea.

Look up these Bible promises: Joshua 1:5; Psalm 32:8; Matthew 10:32; 28:20; John 14:3, 13, 23; 15:5. Write them on slips of paper and place one promise under every plate. During the meal, have each person look under his or her plate and read the promise. Discuss what it means.

Table Talk:

- Fortunes are humorous guesses about what might happen in the future, but they rarely come true. Why?
- Bible promises are fact. How do you know that what God says will come true?

Vitamins and Minerals:

[Joshua said,] "You know with all your heart and soul that not one of all the good promises the LORD your God gave you has failed" (Joshua 23:14).

---

1. Evangelistic Foods, PO Box 16410, Minneapolis, MN 55416, 800-743-0142, http://www.script cookie.com.
2. Lisa Bramen, "The History of Chopsticks," Food and Think, Smithsonian Media, http://blogs.smith sonianmag.com/food/2009/08/the-history-of-chopsticks/; "Most Popular Eating Utensils," Semjan and Lermann, July 18, 2011, http://www.grand-insolvency-show.com/2011/07/popular-eating-utensils/.

Bible Riddles

Mealtime Prayer:

Pray the shortest prayer in the Bible: "Lord, help me!" (Matthew 15:25).

Appetizer:

Play Bible trivia with your family, teaming younger children with a parent. Rules:

1. Take turns making up and asking trivia questions. (You must know the answer!)
2. Start with easy questions.
3. Don't keep points or compare yourselves with others. Instead, enjoy how much you've learned about God's Word!

Bible Trivia Night:

Fix a meal of biblical foods, such as bread and fish (Matthew 15:36), and honey (Exodus 33:3), figs (Nehemiah 13:15), and grapes (Numbers 13:20).

Before you eat, ask the Bible riddle found in Judges 14:14. Don't give away the answer before it's time! Do you know the answer? (Honey from a lion!—see Judges 14:9.)

Table Talk:

- Why is it important to know God's Word?
- What's different from the way you live today and the way the people of the Bible lived? What's the same?
- Do you know any riddles? Share them with your family.

Vitamins and Minerals:

Let the wise listen and add to their learning . . . for understanding proverbs and parables, the sayings and riddles of the wise (Proverbs 1:5–6).

Home on the Range

Mealtime Prayer:

"It's been a long day, We're dusty and tired. This grub smells better than most! We bow down our heads, Give thanks for this food, For in nature, God is our host."

Appetizer:

Plan a camping trip, or set up a tent in your backyard. Take a deep breath. What do you smell? What do you hear? Build a campfire if you have a pit and it's safe, or start a grill. Cook hot dogs, beans, and s'mores.

Camping Trip:

When you're finished eating, go on a nature hike or a walk in the park. (Watch where you're stepping! Keep your eyes open for scat, or animal droppings.) Use these questions as a guide:

Q: How many different shaped leaves can you find? Which is your favorite? Why?

Q: What clues prove that animals have visited this place?

Q: Examine a flower and count the details that make it unique (number of petals, shape, size, stem, colors, etc.).

Table Talk:

When you come back around the tent, answer these questions:

- How are God's qualities clearly seen in what He has made?
- What did you learn about God tonight? (Examples: He pays attention to detail. He loves color and texture.)
- How can you thank God for what He has made?

Vitamins and Minerals:

Since the creation of the world God's invisible qualities—his eternal power and divine nature—have been clearly seen, being understood from what has been made, so that men are without excuse (Romans 1:20).

Hooray for Grandparents!

Mealtime Prayer:

*"Thank You, Lord, that You never change. You loved us yesterday.
You love us today. And You'll love us for every tomorrow. Amen."*

Appetizer:

Did you know that Big Macs were invented in 1968?[1] How old
were your grandparents then? Can your grandparents name the
ingredients of a Big Mac? (Two all-beef patties, special sauce, lettuce,
cheese, pickles, onions, on a sesame-seed bun!)

Grandparent Night:

Invite your grandparents or other older guests over for dinner. Ask them about
the changes they have seen in their lifetimes.

No matter how things change over the years, who never changes? How is
God's care for you now the same as it will be when you're older? Read Isaiah 46:4.

Table Talk:

Ask your grandparents these questions:
- What was your favorite meal as a child? What's your favorite meal now?
- What new appliances do you use today?
- What is one way God has taken care of you over the years? How does
  God take care of you now?

For the kids:
- What types of food do you think you'll eat when you're 75?
- What types of appliances do you think you'll use?

Vitamins and Minerals:

Gray hair is a crown of splendor; it is attained by a righteous life (Proverbs 16:31).

---

1. "McDonald's History," About McDonald's, http://www.aboutmcdonalds.com/mcd/our_company/
mcdonalds_history_timeline.html?DCSext.destination=http://www.aboutmcdonalds.com/mcd/
our_company/mcd_history.html.

Let's Bake

Mealtime Prayer:

Pray: *"O Lord God almighty, who is like You? And who is like me, Your creation?"*
Then thank God for things about yourself that you like.

Appetizer:

Make a recipe card for yourself. What things did God mix together to make
you? What part of you is the icing?

Bake Together:

Plan to bake a treat together, such as cookies or a cake, after your meal. It
doesn't have to be from scratch; a boxed mix will work. Work as a team.

Just as you knew what you were going to bake, God knew you from the
beginning. Read Psalm 139:15–16. Who knows the number of your days? Read
Colossians 1:16. Who were you created for? How do you bring God pleasure?

Table Talk:

- How does baking something special make you feel?
- How do you think God felt when He created you?
- What can you do to make your special treat even more unique? Try it.

Vitamins and Minerals:

You created my inmost being; you knit me together in my mother's womb.
(Psalm 139:13).

Rainbow Salad

Mealtime Prayer:

"Be present at our table, Lord. Be here and everywhere adored. Thy creatures bless, and grant that we may feast in paradise with Thee."[1]

Appetizer:

Did you know that there's a rainbow in heaven? Read Revelation 4:3. What circles God's throne? (Answer: a rainbow, which looks like an emerald)

Picnic:

Plan an outdoor picnic for your family. If it's colder weather, lay out a picnic blanket in your living room. Prepare fruit for a rainbow salad. Before the meal, have family members take turns mixing one of each color:

Red: strawberries, watermelon, or cherries; orange: orange slices or cantaloupe; yellow: bananas or peaches; green: apples or honeydew melon; Blue: blueberries; purple: grapes or blackberries.

Add whipped cream to your salad and enjoy!

The rainbow is a promise from God. Read Genesis 9:9–13. What was God's promise? Whom did God give the promise to? How does this promise affect us today?

Table Talk:

- God always keeps His promises. What are some of these promises?
- How does knowing that God's promises are reliable help you?
- What is your favorite color of the rainbow? Why?

Vitamins and Minerals:

[God said,] "I have set my rainbow in the clouds, and it will be the sign of the covenant between me and the earth" (Genesis 9:13).

---

1. John Cennick, "Be Present at Our Table, Lord," 1741, http://www.hymntime.com/tch/htm/b/p/o/ bpotlord.htm.

Sweet Treat

Mealtime Prayer:

Pray this Bible verse: *"How sweet are your words to my taste, sweeter than honey to my mouth!"* (Psalm 119:103).

Appetizer:

Did you know that jelly beans, gumdrops, and jawbreakers were invented in the late 1800s during the penny-candy craze? Did you know that there are 40 official Jelly Belly flavors made year-round? New flavors are constantly trying to break in. Some of those are kiwi, caramel corn, and French vanilla.[1] What flavor would you invent?

Dessert Devotion:

Place a bowl of jelly beans (or other small candy) in the center of the table for dessert. Have each person eat one piece. What does it taste like? How does it make your mouth feel?

How do kind words sweeten our hearts like candy sweetens our mouths? Read Proverbs 12:25. What does a kind word do?

Now it's time to practice this! Have each person take a turn saying something nice about the family member to his or her left. After one round, switch and go the opposite direction. For each compliment, take two jelly beans.

Table Talk:

- How do kind words make you feel?
- What was your favorite compliment? Why?
- How many compliments can you try to give in one day?

Vitamins and Minerals:

Therefore encourage one another and build each other up, just as in fact you are doing (1 Thessalonians 5:11).

---

1. "About Jelly Belly: Company History," Jelly Belly, http://www.jellybelly.com/about_jelly_belly/company_history.aspx.

Whatcha Watchin'?

Mealtime Prayer:

> *"Lord, strengthen me so that my eyes watch what is good, my heart loves what is good, and my actions display what is good. Amen."*

Appetizer:

Did you know that in 1954, C. A. Swanson and Sons came up with a frozen meal that could easily be heated and eaten in front of the television? It was a complete turkey dinner with cornbread and dressing and gravy.[1] What is your favorite TV dinner?

TV Dinner:

Fix TV dinners, and watch a favorite movie. A good choice is a full-length family film such as *The Lion, the Witch, and the Wardrobe* or *The Muppets* movie. Pay close attention and discuss the film afterward.

- What was the funniest or best part?
- Who was your favorite character? Why?
- Who showed good character? Who showed bad character?
- What's one thing in this movie that would please God?

Table Talk:

- What was one good example from the movie?
- People watch you just as you watch the examples of others. What can you do to be a good example?
- Who are you an example for?

Vitamins and Minerals:

Don't let anyone look down on you because you are young, but set an example for the believers in speech, in life, in love, in faith and in purity (1 Timothy 4:12).

---

1. "Invention Trivia," InventHelp, 2012, http://www.inventhelp.com/Invention-trivia_9.asp.

FOCUS ON THE FAMILY®

Welcome to the Family ——

Whether you purchased this book, borrowed it, or received it as a gift, thanks for reading it! This is just one of many insightful, biblically based resources that Focus on the Family produces for people in all stages of life.

Focus is a global Christian ministry dedicated to helping families thrive as they celebrate and cultivate God's design for marriage and experience the adventure of parenthood. Our outreach exists to support individuals and families in the joys and challenges they face, and to equip and empower them to be the best they can be.

Through our many media outlets, we offer help and hope, promote moral values and share the life-changing message of Jesus Christ with people around the world.

Focus on the Family MAGAZINES

These faith-building, character-developing publications address the interests, issues, concerns, and challenges faced by every member of your family from preschool through the senior years.

For More INFORMATION

 ONLINE:
Log on to
FocusOnTheFamily.com
In Canada, log on to
FocusOnTheFamily.ca

PHONE:
Call toll-free:
**800-A-FAMILY
(232-6459)**
In Canada, call toll-free:
800-661-9800

THRIVING FAMILY®	FOCUS ON	FOCUS ON	FOCUS ON
Marriage & Parenting	THE FAMILY	THE FAMILY	THE FAMILY
	CLUBHOUSE JR.®	CLUBHOUSE®	CITIZEN®
	Ages 4 to 8	Ages 8 to 12	U.S. news issues

Rev. 3/11

Start an adventure!
with Focus on the Family

Whether you're looking for new ways to teach young children about God's Word, entertain active imaginations with exciting adventures or help teenagers understand and defend their faith, we can help. For trusted resources to help your kids thrive, visit our online Family Store at:

FocusOnTheFamily.com/resources